BLACK TULIPS

BLACK TULIPS

MOYA PACEY

RECENT
WORK
PRESS

Black Tulips
Recent Work Press
Canberra, Australia

Copyright © Moya Pacey 2017

National Library of Australia
Cataloguing-in-Publication entry.

Pacey, Moya
Black Tulips/ Moya Pacey

ISBN: 9780648087823(paperback)

All rights reserved. This book is copyright. Except for private study,
research, criticism or reviews as permitted under the Copyright Act,
no part of this book may be reproduced, stored in a retrieval system, or
transmitted in any form by any means without prior written permission.
Enquiries should be addressed to the publisher.

Cover illustration: 'Tulip' by Revolution540 reproduced under Creative
Commons Attribution 2.0 Generic Licence
Cover design: Recent Work Press
Author Picture by Jonquil Mackey, 2017
Set in Bembo Std

recentworkpress.com

for my family

Contents

Reading Shakespeare in the dark	1
My whole family sits on top of the sideboard	2
Monkey puzzle tree	3
Red shoes	4
I'll never come back	5
Sing your landay	6
The contents of her handbag	7
At the Beaumont-Hamel Memorial, France	8
Follower	9
Does the nun know?	10
Aphasia	11
Sugihara	12
Featherfall	13
At La Forge	14
At the Holy Well	15
Between Sitges and Barcelona	16
Last touch in Barcelona	17
Building fire	18
Crucifix	19
Egg zen	20
Hide and seek at the Memorial to the Murdered Jews of Europe, Berlin	21
I'd drive across three moors	22
Poor man's farthing	23
Knitting for insomniacs	24
Sacred	25
Linguicide	26
Makeover	27
Tourist guides	28
Harbour	29
After looking through Carver's 'window'	30
Mind and soul	31

MRI	32
Palimpsest	33
Nesting	34
Imposter	35
Proofs of existence	36
Quarrel	37
She leaves him behind in aisle nine	38
Romance	39
Red linoleum	40
Snake	41
The calligrapher's breath	42
After her dad passed away	43
The lost cow	44
The collector	45
Silver fugue	46
The woman carries an aid box on her head	47
The woman who tries to keep her distance	48
Jogbra	49
Violin	50
From the artist's cleaning lady	51
Larkman	52
Rahroon Westmeath	53
False identity	54
Gate	55
I packed my mother away like winter	56
Leavetaking	57
She'd rather break than bend	58
Glazier	59
Afterword	60

Out of the wood of thoughts that grows by night.

Edward Thomas

Reading Shakespeare in the dark

Today is being kept at a distance.
It's waiting outside on the street
for us to open the heavy curtains
unlock the front door
let it into the house.
It will come in with a wooden coffin
mourners in crisp white shirts, black ties,
pressed suits and soft words.

We loved that man.

The girl is reading Shakespeare in the dark.
The Dream's nearly done
Oberon has won and soon she will close
the final page, get out of her grandmother's bed
take off her nightdress
tie back her red hair with a blue ribbon
put on a new black dress and unlock the door.
Just not yet.

My whole family sits on top of the sideboard

(Summer holiday, Hornsea, UK 1961)

We don't look comfortable perched
as if we all want to be somewhere else.
My brother's sitting side on, giving us
his wannabe rock star pose
planning a future far away from the sideboard.

I sit next to him, my face square on to the camera
wearing a tiny frown between my brows
worrying and crossing my fingers and trying
to remember the name of the saint I need
to pray to for a Happy Family.

My sister's body twists and her green
eyes search for another family she'd rather
sit with. The baby is a baby and believes
dad when he says how lucky we are to be
sitting on top of the sideboard this summer
holiday in Hornsea in 1961.

Dad's got it wrong. You can see it on mam's face.
She's not smiling and she's wearing a jumper
and a mac instead of a frock and silk stockings,
and she wants to get off the sideboard.

Monkey puzzle tree

Monkey puzzles need the space of privilege
become status symbols grown in gardens
owned by couples called Nigel and Pamela
who live on avenues and have
fish ponds and fountains; fancy perennials.
Always a paved terrace with a view beyond
the wisteria and the ha-ha for the Nigels
and Pamelas to sit and drink Pimms
summer afternoons with friends and discuss
whose turn it is to host the village fête.

A man comes once a week by bicycle.
He unclips his trouser bottoms, tips
his cap and does the necessary:
oils the lawnmower, weeds the herbaceous
border, pots up seedlings and after
his labours he stands and marvels
at the monkey puzzle tree splendid
in the middle of the newly-mown lawn.

Red shoes

They walk me out of my seventeen-years
down a boulevard where I'm unknown
but intéressante. I have a new name.
The priest frowns and asks, 'What saint
is called Scarlet for God's sake?'
I say these shoes don't belong to a Mary.
They have a sole like a park full of cherry
blossoms and a tongue made for kissing.
Red lips practise blowing smoke rings
in my apartment on the sixth floor
of the eighth arrondissement—I rent
for a song—la patronne sees my red shoes
and knows I am full of savoir faire—
the right sort of girl she wants there—
a jeune fille wearing shoes red
as the velvet tasselled curtains at L'Opéra
opening and closing every night.

I'll never come back

to bend low
crouch beside you
on the street in Kolkata where
you wash clothes
in a plastic bowl—
small and red.
                      See your smile.

I'll never come back
to see women and children
squatting on saris, in darkness
                      outside Howrah Station.
To step over the body at my feet
ascend the iron staircase spiralling.

I'll never come back
at dawn to Varanasi to watch the train
of women—each one standing beneath a water pump,
lifting saris from their heads, loosening plaits of hair.
A black river cascading along the platform.

Sing your landay

In the dark cage of the village
a woman's voice sings of the girl
who stole her brothers' honour.
They shaved her black curls,
closed her green eyes, scooped
the body into a sack
threw it into the cold river.

Come back into the world
girl with black curls and green eyes.
Put on your wedding shoes.
Let your hennaed fingers
beat the hand drum.
Sing your landay
over and over.

The contents of her handbag

A cotton handkerchief of the cheapest kind
bought in a pack of twelve at the bazaar.
The guard raises its whiteness skywards
sees through it frail dawn light.
A leather wallet small with notes and coins
for food at the market: *rice, lentils, oranges.*
The guard studies the photograph—her husband—
round cheeks, brown eyes and hair.
Her fingers caught in it that last morning.
He pretended annoyance. *Afifa,*
you have made my hair untidy.
He crossed to the chipped mirror hanging
on the apartment wall, took a comb
from his tunic pocket, and ran it through
his hair, and (as was his habit) checked
his teeth for any stray pomegranate
seeds. Satisfied, he turned from the mirror.

The guard picks up the woman's lipstick
Crimson Rose. He imagines her lips
beneath the veil. Stares hard. Her eyes.
Two brown rivers kohl-rimmed.
The guard motions for her to put away
the contents of her handbag.
Waves her through the barrier.
She stops midway as if she's forgotten something.

Opens up her handbag.

A blast of air shreds the veil.
Her eyes net golden
mesmerising light.

At the Beaumont-Hamel Memorial, France

The boy's letter hangs straight on the pale wall,
'Don't cry, Mary, this way we won't starve
I promise I'll be home for Christmas.'
His penmanship upright and precise.
Steady hands that Somme morning pulling
on bright blue puttees; fingering
his caribou insignia and pleased
that he doesn't stink of fish.

He wants to be gone over the top
with the other eight-hundred Newfies—
farmers and fishermen—
dead men who stepped out
heads bent; chins tucked in
against the fierce snow of battle.

Follower

Five men and a boy smear zinc on cheeks and noses,
preparing for a day's fishing as if it were war
especially Jo-Jo.
His father sends him running up the beach
for a yellow bucket full of stinking prawns.

Last night, the men lit loud campfires,
burned steaks, looted stubbies from giant eskies.
Inside domed tents their wives hushed babies,
drank white wine and unhooked the day.

The boy hid in the paperbarks beneath
a star-filled sky and heard five men's
secrets. This morning his father warns:
'Watch it, loose-lips.'

Jo-Jo twists and turns on the fish-spotter's seat,
he wants to be
gone
                              over the restless bar.

Does the nun know?

Does the nun know as she twists
bleached cotton to and fro
sturdy fingers moving bobbins
with such steady precision,
pinning her lace fast
to a small pillow placed
soft upon her flattened knees.
Is there a glimmer of understanding
how her lace scallops, delicate
as a sea creature's empty shell
stranded on a frothy tide,
will be sewn around the silken edge
of another woman's bed-pillow
to spread her hair just so?
How that other woman's body
lifts and falls to show,
oh, with such coquettish grace.
'Slow, slow,' that other woman says.
No, wait.
Does the nun know
where her lace will go?

Aphasia

She is dumb as any metal
locked and fastened down with all the words
she knows she used to know.

Words fat as honey bees with golden pollen
bee-hived in her brain.
Words she loved.

Words she had for all the green spaces:
leas and glades, rills and birch woods.
She wants to say, she saw this morning:

black tulips—their bullet heads bending
low, low to the paved terrace;
giving up their weight of petals.

Sugihara

His right hand grips the pen
dips in and out of the inkpot—
marks the sheet of white paper
   bold with black characters.

Forgive me
I pity them
I gave them the visas
I wish them the best ...

On the train, Mother pulls the baby close,
makes room so Grandfather can rest.
Father checks his pocket, pats
   the visa safe in his wallet.

In the darkness outside: no camps
no chimneys or barbed wire fences.
Mother unfastens her coat, loosens
   the scarf tight at her throat.

Featherfall

days afterwards we find
feathers everywhere
one in my hair
one in my purse
amongst the small change
strange
the nurse finds one
hidden in her pocket
another tucked inside
the baby's blanket
an old woman reminisces
just like the day war ended
peace fell softly as kisses.

At La Forge

She wants to be left
alone in the overgrown garden.
Refuses to join us each day to drive
lanes of poplars and plane trees.
She isn't tempted by our stories,
wine, food and laughter or
marrons golden with bees.

She picks up a pair of kitchen scissors
to use as secateurs (there are no garden
tools in the holiday house).
Her small white hands hold the steel
firm and snip and slice
into the wild garden.

One day when we return,
heads full of sunflowers and chateaus,
she's sitting smoking a cigarette.
She points to a grotto
grey stone, mossy-veined.
Behind the tangle, she's found
a nest empty of birds—
exposed like a secret.

At the Holy Well

(Fore Abbey, County Westmeath, Ireland)

My Irish aunts lounge against the blessèd stones
loving the way heat sculpts their cold bones.
They recite by heart a litany of holy places
where they've followed the lame and blind.

They've collected medals blessed by six popes,
plenary indulgences, each has a scapular
hidden between her skinny breasts.

The way the rain's keeping off's a miracle.

Talking now and then of this and that
my Irish aunts lean in towards each other
hands pushed deep into the pockets
of mackintoshes, fingering beads;
counting out the decades
of a joyful mystery—
punctuating the silence
                with unspoken aves.

Between Sitges and Barcelona

The man lying on the track is taking his time dying.
Blue lights flash and uniforms crowd but inside
the train no-one complains or demands
that the train starts up and moves on.

No-one walks up and down impatient or angry.
There's no looking at wristwatches or shouting
into mobile phones. Women wearing black
keep each other company and finger rosaries.

The driver sits on the top rung of the carriage steps,
head cradled in his arms. One by one,
men from the train take it in turns to step
down and stand beside him. They place

one hand on his hunched shoulder as if
to press upon him words they don't say:
He crossed the tracks without looking.
You're not responsible.

I want to pray as the locals do. Instead
I think of you and remember the nurse said
I'd know you were gone when the last breath left.
I watched. Waited as each one stretched

further and further between us in the little room.

Last touch in Barcelona

When the swallow falls
one wing fanned
skimming
the other broken
desperate to beat air
to rise and leave this earth
the driver stops the number fifty bus
leaves the wheel
steps down and kneels
spreads his hands
wide like calloused stars
bows his head
picks up the bird
places it beneath a plane tree
with a murmured Spanish blessing.

I think of that last touch.
The driver's rasp of skin
on the swallow's broken wing.

Building fire

My mother takes an axe
to wood the colour of cold honey,
splinters, kindles,
twists last night's 'Gazette'
into paper sticks;
takes a match from the box
strikes and lights
the cardinal points
coaxes fire;
blows with lipsticked lips.
Fire quickens …

My mother shows me how to trap
hot air.
She props a shovel—
blade rested on the iron fender—
drapes last night's newspaper
across its wooden shaft.

She makes a vacuum …

If there's no wood, she'll burn
old shoes—one winter
she chopped the upright piano
we played chopsticks on, piece
by shiny wooden piece—
What happened to the ivories?

Fire ignites
spreads a singe of ink and paper
flicks a blade of flame
slashes the skin of last night's news.
Pulls away the shovel.

Crucifix

(for John)

Dad says if we kiss the wooden cross
each night we'll be safe
upstairs, where we wait for white
sleep to come beyond
the stairwell and brass rods,
that hold the slip and slide of carpet
steady for our tread.
Downstairs a girl, who is our mother,
combs black curls, hums ivory tunes
off key. Her feet tap time.

We don't know the heavy-doored
church where one day we'll push
full weight against its bulk of wood.
We won't enter yet.
We're staying safe upstairs.
We've kissed the wooden cross.
Dad says if black sleep comes,
tonight the cross will save us.

Egg zen

(for Kate)

Yolked to life
the sun is a perfect O
risen in this blue morning.

Newly-laid in clean yellow straw
a brown egg passive and perfect
settled at the temperature of my blood.

I wish I were as blank of history
as this zero of egg
cupped in my palm.

After time turns upside down
measures four minutes and thirty seconds,
I spoon mindfulness into my mouth.

Hide and seek at the Memorial to the Murdered Jews of Europe, Berlin

Inga, Inga ...
A small boy jumps out
blocks the narrow path.

'Are you ok?' He nods.
Vanishes beyond
where thirteen paths lead

onto a snatch of sunlight.
Inga, Inga ...
Seeking his sister hidden beneath

two thousand seven hundred and eleven grey stones.

Six million names called each day.

I'd drive across three moors

Cocooned in her car seat,
that last summer drive,
my mother, her skin worn
too thin fell finely from
the cradle of her bones.

Time ran a trickle
of old blood in her quiet
veins. Sinead sang
a lullaby so soft
on the radio.

Beneath blue sky
over three Jurassic moors
we drove dumb
no other car in sight.
Sealed inside we watched
the moors fall to dales
Danby, Egton, Glaisdale.
The sun rose high.

I needed the day to keep;
for the saxe blue sky and purple heather
to stay strung out light
not alter to the heavy dark.
But somewhere off the world changed.

Flit, flicker, quiver, stir
a brown lacewing frets
the thready air settles
on a white hibiscus
fine as oriental paper.

Poor man's farthing

Last thing at night before he went to bed
dad emptied his pockets of
shillings, sixpences, threepenny bits,
pennies and halfpennies. Sometimes
a poor man's farthing or two.
Heads and tails they lay upon the table.
Never counted in neat columns or piles.
Dad said he was glad to be rid:
'All this slack weighs my pockets down.'

He was a man who wanted to be free
of the worry of rent and bills.
Fond of quoting Mr Micawber—
'Happiness is sixpence to spare.
Misery sixpence over budget.'

Shares rise and fall. Every day
the FTSE and the NASDQ work their magic.

Dad left his pile of coins on the table
locked the door and went up to bed.

Knitting for insomniacs

On nights when sleep eludes
women across the world
pick up needles—gather

dropped stitches of spite
and old hatreds—
untangle the skeins of war.

They knit soft bombs.
Cover a tank with pink wool,
hang a strawberry

tassel from its turret.
Swathe a submarine
yellow with acrylic and cotton

warm as a baby's bootee.
Fat pom-poms conceal
                          the dark hull.

Sacred

The medics have haloed Mohammed's head.
Eyes closed, he lies still as a marble saint

in a medieval cathedral.
Arms outstretched, the technician steadies

a metal plate ready for the x-ray photograph
eyes intent on the large lamp

lighting upon Mohammed's torso.
All life is sacred

whether you are friend or foe
in the field hospital at Kandahar.

Linguicide

The soldiers throw the books on the stove
take pleasure in seeing words burn.
After that, the new hard consonants lodge

in people's throats like fish-bones they can't
rid themselves of no matter how they clear
their throats and try to swallow. Tongues

thicken and lose their facility to click.
Vowels slide and letters disappear
from the alphabet. There are official decrees,

executions. Some commit whole books
a poem, a prayer, to memory. Words
linger as faint footprints at the shoreline

until the tide washes them away. One old woman
has the word for that feeling when skin tingles (after
particularly cold weather). When she dies it is gone.

Makeover

Forgive the absence of your beloved ivy
wild on the sagging wooden fence. I
tugged and tugged, but they were
inseparable.

Forgive the absence of your sweet pittosporum
feral with lorikeets feasting on loud
blossom, the frenzy of fruit.

Forgive the absence of your dear agave
one for each of our children
grown tall and unrestrained.
Never flowered.

I've moved them out of sight.
Four staked standard floribunda—
icebergs in their place.

Tourist guides

Outside Kensington Palace, two policemen
tell the couple with the pushchair
(who might have a bomb hidden in there,
under the baby). *No. Hamleys
is on Regent Street but Harrods is quite near.*
They clutch sub-machine guns to their breasts.
Smile like awful mothers.

Harbour

Walking home after the show, they stop
beneath the bridge to wonder—
the harbour lit up like a stage.
Night ferries and a cruise ship
blaze with light and travellers.

The full moon spots them
waiting for their cue. Downstage
a fisherman patient at his line.
Two lovers in the wings: heads
close, bare arms wrapped
around each others' waists.

On into the jasmine heat-filled night
they walk, unsure what will happen next.
Unrehearsed, fireworks burst.
His hand touches hers
                moves quickly apart.

Not lovers then?

After looking through Carver's 'window'

Spotted gums prod the sky
like diviners' rods
exploring out there.

Two crimson rosellas scatter
sunflower seeds spilling
a sapphire throated bowl of sound.

When will the rains come?
Your face turns away.
Things stand as they stood before.

Mind and soul

(for Brian)

You and I sit on blue canvas chairs
so still and quiet we might be posing
for an important photograph.
But there's no camera,
only mugs of hot coffee,
two apple muffins on a wooden table.

A small white butterfly feeds from a yellow flower—
with petals so slight that the butterfly
stills its quiver,
extracting nectar.
Yellow flower, white butterfly
in perfect equipoise

When I point out the butterfly and flower,
I almost hear the flutter of your mind
unfurl and shake out knowledge
you have folded away and want
to open up and tell me—
about monarch butterflies and their warm migrations.

My head inclines towards yours—
I tell you the ancient Greeks had a word for butterfly—
the place where mind and soul meet.

MRI

Wrap your body in the blue paper smock.
Stay as warm as possible. And calm.
Look at the seascape hanging on the bare wall.
A ball of yellow sun.
A cloudless sky.
Think of the summer day you lay
drowsy on dry sand wet
after a birthday swim.
Tell yourself a birthday will come again.
Time now.
Leave the cubicle—
step outside and enter
                            the machine.

Palimpsest

The stiff starch of the hospital
sheet will not mould white

to her. The prickle of the pillow-
slip digs into the nape of her neck

bruises soft behind each ear.
Each touch of linen an incision.

Scraped clean her world's a ream
of paper.

Nesting

Some birds crave the touch of soft,
love the pleasures of rabbit fur,
feathers and downy ferns.
Hanker for honey myrtle
or bind grasses and sheep's wool.
Others like a bit of rough and risk,
the threat of crevices in stone walls,
companions with dangerous reputations,
birds of prey and wasps.
Not the crested pigeon,
her frail nest rests
waiting on a tremor.
She's poised
to whirr up
                      flight and flee.

Imposter

She's not playing bingo with the others.
She's searching for her name.
She knows the one they laminated,
fixed on a card above her narrow bed,
belongs to someone else.

Her feet slippered in soft-pink
felt—marked with black texta:
L for left and R for right.
NOT TO BE LAUNDERED.

Scissored neatly into her skull—
her hair's completely white.
The left collar of her pale blue blouse
sticks up like a crumpled wing.

'To my darling Lily'.
Dancing with Ron in their wedding photo,
she's in profile, black and white, red-
headed, gamine like Audrey Hepburn
in 'Breakfast at Tiffany's'.

*I'm not Lily. My name is
something else. Something sexy.*

Proofs of existence

Church of Domine Quo Vadis,
Appian Way, Rome

Jesus & St Peter's footsteps
in Domine Quo Vadis.
Twenty toes & four soles
impressed into sandstone.

They might be shepherds' feet
or Roman soldiers
returning from war,
or the masons who built the church,
needing to leave evidence
as lovers do—
carving hearts into trees & rocks.

Most likely vestiges
sprung from mishaps.
Perhaps, two impatient people
stepped on the still
wet mortar & told a story
to cover their mistake.

Quarrel

When the sulphur-crested cockatoo falls from its roost it makes a sound
like nothing we've ever heard.
Left wing spread, right wing folded under its breast, neck broken,
one eye half-open, tongue balled like a nut in its beak.

We look for the wound that dropped it from our roof,
but find none. Why this moment to fall,
to stop our quarrel dead before we can find words to say we're sorry.
It might be an omen of our own deaths.

We box the bird. Give our fear a burial.
You take the spade and ask, 'Where shall I dig the hole?'
After rain the earth's receptive.

The cockatoo is our albatross,
we keep bringing it on board
knowing when we do,

how it will end.
You in one box.
Me in another.

She leaves him behind in aisle nine

He's checking every tin of baked
beans, every jar of golden honey
for value for money, juggling
three jars of pasta sauce:
Select, Dolmio, Homebrand.

Once he'd held her in his arms
seduced by her charms
now he fingers apples and pears
inspecting every imperfection,
before he makes a careful selection.

When he refuses to pay
for Belgian paté, she leaves
him behind in aisle nine tut-tutting
at the cost of French Camembert—

Romance

He's all leather and slouch
breath like cinders in my ear;
slivers of crescent moons
grime beneath his fingernails.

I liked that last one, you say
so did your father. Lovely manners
on him and a real way with words.

In the wood, shadows fall
beyond roads and rail lines. Dark
crescent moons stroke my golden
hair; press the flesh of my milk-white neck.

Mark my words, he'll never settle.
That sort never does. This one,
well … It's your funeral.

No mention of the fox cub
in the wood, searching for her mother.

Red linoleum

I am always going back to that place
Where my seven-year old face
won't fit the too-small mirror fixed
over the chipped stone sink.
I need to pin back my fringe
stop it falling into my eyes
fasten it with a kirby grip.
I push fingers through my hair
wash my hands with a slip of Sunlight Soap
dry them on a cotton towel hanging
from a nail on the back of the green door.
I am always going back to that place
Where water's cold in summer
the boiler unlit; sticky papers fastened
on the ceiling to catch a buzz of flies.
Where the blue glass of flame's switched
off, the saucepan still warm
and butter melts in the marbled larder.
I am always going back to that place
to stand on red linoleum.

Snake

(for S.E.)

We're in a kind of dream this morning
sitting upstream in the shallow river—
summer air hot on our skins.
You face me but your gaze turns inwards.
Beyond your head, sky and mountains fall
into the place where all merges into blue.
Inert as a river stone you're unaware
of the long ripple stopping at your neck. Snake
raises its bullet head—bronze eyes unblinking.
Will it leave the cool water to bask,
to stretch its brown body, to warm cold blood
on your head mistaking you for stone?
Snake!
Where?
Arms, hands, legs, feet push upright.
Sway, stumble. When I look back,
you're on your knees
splashing and turning. Your eyes
       searching everywhere.

The calligrapher's breath

The calligrapher
pauses between
bone and air
spine curved
lungs heavy
his brush a quietened
left wing feather
presses
strokes
spines an arc
expires

After her dad passed away

She saw him on Google Earth coming out of the house.
It was a sign she said. It was his way of saying, 'I'm alright.'
She said it was nice for her mother. The way dad was smiling
waving at the camera on his way to work. She said it was typical.
He was quite a funny man.

The lost cow

All night we hear her call,
see the beam of our neighbour's
torchlight sweeping the paddocks
looking for their lost cow. This morning
you ask, 'Are you thinking of a poem?'
'Yes, I'm going to call it, *The lost cow.*'

I'll write about all the losses: socks, loose
coins fallen behind soft-cushioned sofas,
shoes looped around lamp posts, laces dangling
like nooses, keys, coins, wallets, names and numbers,
passports and purses, pens, phones, glasses, gloves.

Then the people we lose along the way some
deliberately, when they turn a corner, we go straight on.
We don't wait. They have the map.

This afternoon I stand on the veranda—
no other house in sight and the metal gate
at the end of the driveway's locked. You're
gone and last night's lost cow's grazing. Content
to be found unlike the native pigeon
hiding in the thick of callistemons.

The collector

Through a cloud of flies in Brazil. On face, hair, hands and neck. Reminds me of Bud Junior's breath on my cheek holding him close, rocking him to sleep on a hot August night down on the Delta. I reckon, now he's grown, he'd like to see my Trophy Room on a summer's afternoon—the way yellow shines in and lights up the steel pins and my Prussian Blue. I haven't seen him since he was two.

His mother said she was going down the mall to buy him new sneakers and that was the last I saw of them. I got letters from lawyers postmarked 'Detroit'. No contact, the judge said. His mother said stuff—some of it true but a lot of it she talked up. It wasn't right. I think my boy would forgive. I've written in my will, flies, steel pins, rosewood-cases, green-baize cloths. Bud Junior gets the lot.

Silver fugue

The fishmonger ices silver salmon
arranges each fish on marble tiers.

Like a miser caressing his pile of coins:
stacking sixpences, shillings, half and

full crowns into steady piles.
The mother strokes her child's head

straightens the tinsel halo,
lying crooked over his left eye.

The child stands with the angel choir—
a careful scale arranged on wooden rows.

'Tall ones at the back, small ones at the front.'

Like a shoal of silver fish they wait.
Mouths open caught on the hook of sound.

The woman carries an aid box on her head

Dressed in a shapeless abaya
she is neither young nor old.
The cardboard box has moulded to the shape

of her black-veiled head, she holds it steady
right arm extended, narrow wrist exposed,
fingers at full stretch.

Her face uncovered and her gaze calm
unhurried she turns to the camera,
eyes narrowed against the light.

Behind her in the photograph, men
walk along an ancient road
towards the open gate of the refugee camp.

The men wear jeans and warm jackets.
Some have hoods pulled around their faces
others bareheaded. All empty handed.

The scene might belong in a book of bible stories.
The story in which the woman goes to the well
balancing a ewer of water on her head.

The one where she meets a Good Samaritan.

The woman who tries to keep her distance

I expect them to be standoffish—
when I come home
after seven weeks away—
but my cats won't leave me alone.
The Siamese is the worst, curling
around my legs. Miaowing
a long abandonment.
I close the door on the cats
escape into the garden
try to find solace
pulling weeds by the wooden fence.
I'd forgotten my neighbour—
a man who yells profanities
into his mobile phone.
It's hard to weed when language
punches and shoves brutal
consonants through palings.
I straighten up and retreat
indoors to the cats'
sharp-edged cries.
The Siamese claws my ankles.
Draws blood.

Jogbra

'Touch your nose to the floor,'
(says my personal trainer).
Let's see how far down he can get
when I strap two kettle drums to his chest.

When big breasts get moving
the nipples on a C or D cup
accelerate up to forty miles an hour.
Faster than a Ferrari.

Amazons chopped off their right breasts
to hurl spears and shoot arrows straight.

Modern women invest in a jogbra. Think
double jock strap slung around your neck.

Violin

I am close
I can smell you
I part your soft neck skin
You fit me & rest your chin
& push your left cheek into my patina
Hard into my wood & move
Your bow across my belly

Your bow across my belly
Hard into my wood & move
& push your left cheek into my patina
You fit me & rest your chin
I part your soft neck skin
I can smell you
I am close

From the artist's cleaning lady

'Leave things exactly where you find them. Don't polish the mirrors and fetch my straw hat from the yellow room. Put it on my head.'

She goes out of the house onto Duxton Street carrying a bag crammed with paint pots and brushes, a blank canvas tucked under her arm.

I change her bed, clean the loo and bathroom, empty the ashtrays. I can't get the vacuum cleaner into the rooms or open the windows to get rid of cobwebs. She worries a strong wind might carry all this clutter away.

Once I moved her Turkish teapot, and tossed two rotten pomegranates into the bin. 'I don't think we're suited. My house,' she explained, 'is Art.'

Since then, I've learned to lift and dust, ignore the tattered curtains at the windows. I peek and see the sweet wrappers still under the wooden stool in the kitchen and the baking tray's been used as a palette. The blender's full of paint soup. I always bring my own sandwich.

Today she's covered the dining table with a kelim rug, arranged five mandarins in a blue bowl and three clivias in an olive vase.

I touch one of the clivia's hot petals, straighten its green straps of leaves, stroke my fingers over the rug.

Larkman

All the fledgling lark knows is the dark
wooden box nailed shut but for two flaps.
Open they let in the light.
All the larkman knows is a metal cage
lowering into the pit. Coal dust trapped
in his throat and the shaft smothering
warm. Sundays at dawn, he carries the box
up Skircoat Moor and slides back the flaps.

The lark opens its throat and the unboxed
song soars on and on ...
In chapel that night, the larkman snug
in his wooden pew sings, 'Safe evermore
under God's wings'. The lark's song
boxed, folded, tight. The absence of light.

Rahroon Westmeath

They woke, dressed, and climbed down the ladder from the loft. The man cut thick slices of bread from the loaf and they used them to scoop up the eggs and rashers and ate straight from the frypan. They stepped out of the kitchen door into the dark-before-dawn light. The man carrying the lantern, and his turf cutter, led the way across the red bog. He could have crossed it with his eyes shut. The boy followed trusting in his path, wheeling the barrow over the spongy ground.

The man climbed down into the trench, using the iron ladder, and began to nick and cut and slice the turf. He tossed each slab up to the boy, spade ready to lift each one into the barrow. When it was full, the boy wheeled it back to the house. While they worked, the man entertained the boy with his mimicry. He took off a neighbour, well gone with the drink, after a session in Brady's Bar and Fr O'Hara giving out in the pulpit about them all being rotten sinners deserving what was coming to them if they didn't pull their socks up and start living good catholic lives.

The sun rose higher and the boy lost track of the barrow loads he'd ferried. He got to thinking that his task was the harder one and asked the man to swap places. Without another word, the man climbed up the iron ladder and took the boy's place at the barrow. The boy climbed down and picked up the turf cutter. He nicked and cut and sliced the way he'd seen the man do and used all his strength but could only manage to toss three slabs up out of the deep trench.

The man said nothing to the boy but climbed down into the trench and took up where he'd left off with the cutting and the stories and the mimicry. The boy resumed his barrowing until the late afternoon meal of strong sugary tea and slices of white bread thickly spread with blackberry jam.

> the old man recalls
> that day the sweetness
> in everything

False identity

Dad planted onions & hoped for giants
like the ones we saw at the Egton Show
—the year the donkey bit Peter.
I put sixpence in a machine
& got a fortune card.

'You'll go far,' it said.
'As far as here to there,' dad said,
bending double, drilling onions
into rows & singing the Lourdes hymn—
the only one he knew by heart.

We sang it at school & to Bobby,
our blue budgie, last thing at night,
before we covered his cage with
the sunshade off the old pram.

'Peter's the last & there
won't be any more.
Five's enough,' mam said.

Dad let it slip, the night Peter
was born. We were all waiting
in the front room. Mam was upstairs
with the midwife & Aunt Lily.

'This will be our sixth,' dad said.
'Our second was stillborn.'

I think of you my sister.
Alive you might have my name,
& I would be somebody else.

Gate

Our school is not a château but we have a châtelaine,
Sister Mary Hilda swings steel keys
locks us in each morning and out again at four.

At our school, the free milk freezes solid, turns
sour when we warm it at the winter pipes steaming:
pissy knickers, wet mittens and sodden woolly socks.

We eat our dinners at wooden tables, 'Please
don't give Moya custard,' mam writes in her careful
copperplate (learned from her own nuns), 'it makes her sick.'

Wimpleless and headscarved,
my mam stays outside the anvilled gate,
stands in the nunless world and waits

while I am layered and keyed with rosaries,
aves, benedictions and hard novenas.

I packed my mother away like winter

I bring you out of the wardrobe dressed in astrakhan,
foetal curls of black wool that never breathed.
I stroke and stroke and bury my face in your warmth.
Feeling you yield, I lift the heavy collar until it covers
my ears and half my face.
I'm breathing
Soir de Paris, Max Factor, and something else
I try to remember.

I want to say, Mother, I'm sorry
your life wasn't an astrakhan coat.
You needed the accessories—
a purse stuffed with five-pound notes, perfume
from Chanel, an heirloom rope of pearls
evenly matched. You had slim ankles, shining hair,
a necklace studded with blue glass beads,
a golden wedding ring worn thin and five children.

Leavetaking

you rose from your green armchair
and left the room on a summer's afternoon
yellow roses in full bloom
sea salt on the breeze
buttercups in the long grass

She'd rather break than bend

Kingston Glassworks, Canberra 2017

She's sand and fire caught
on the end of the rod. Two men lift,

carry, push her deep into the furnace.
Melting fast her core softens. Before

she hardens the men work fast,
rolling, dipping, turning, tweezing,

paddling until she's ready to be sheared
free. She's fish. Orange. Precise.

Glazier

After he knocks off work Saturday afternoon, he rides his pushbike to Pearsons for a pane of glass, straps it to the crossbar and wheels it home along the Greenway. The weather's fine because it's summer when my brother kicks his football through our front room window.

No-one else about. Just me standing outside on the garden path reaching my hand through the empty frame to take some putty from his hand, our fingers touching. I roll mine into a sticky pellet liking the oily smell of linseed so much I sniff and sniff. Dad's inside spreading his. Smoothing it with the knife borrowed from the kitchen.

Frowning and biting down on his lower lip, green eyes narrowing he holds the pane steady, arms outstretched, big hands gripping both sides, lifting and taking its weight. He stops humming. Pushes the glass gently into the frame. A bony elbow pokes out from the hole unravelling in his grey woollen jumper.

I don't say anything. I don't want the glass to fall and shatter.

The last time I see him, he's at the station standing on the very edge of the crowd. Head bowed. Arms hanging at his side. The coach engine's revving. My knuckles rap-rapping on the window.

> no goodbye
> between us
> rain smears the pane

Afterword

Black Tulips are symbols of mystery and elegance and are hard to grow—a bit like writing poems. There is always a sense of mystery around how a poem makes it on to the page. How it sits beneath the surface as a garden bulb does until the conditions are right for it to begin to sprout and push into being.

Once the poem is on the page, there's the challenge of shaping. Finding a form. The search for the best words in the best order. Even ordinary words take on new meanings. There is always tension between using the precision tools and techniques of poetry and the decision to let the poem go its own way.

Notes

p. 3, 'Monkey puzzle tree', Araucaria araucana is an evergreen tree native to Southern Chile and Western Argentina. It is the hardiest species of conifer.

p. 6, 'Sing your landay', inspired by reading 'I am the Beggar of the World: Landays from Contemporary Afghanistan', trans. by Eliza Griswold (Farrar Strauss and Giroux, 2015).

p. 8, 'At the Beaumont-Hamel Memorial, France', it was a magnificent display of trained and disciplined valour, and its assault only failed of success because dead men can advance no further—the epigram said of the actions of the 1st Newfoundland Regiment by the Commander of the 29th British Division at the Battle of the Somme.

p. 10, 'Does the nun know?', convents supplemented their incomes by lace making such as the Poor Clares in Kenmare, Co Kerry, Ireland.

p. 12, 'Sugihara', Chiune Sugihara, a Japanese diplomat in Lithuania in 1941, helped Jews leave by issuing them transit visas to Japan.

p. 23, 'Poor man's farthing', 'The poor man's farthing is worth more than all the gold on Africa's shore.' Quote by William Blake, 'Auguries of Innocence'.

p. 43, 'After her dad passed away', a found poem based around the story Rebecca Loughborough told me on a long car journey northward.

p. 49, 'Jogbra', adapted from Amanda Hess | Jul 16, 2013 ESPN the Magazine.

p. 51, 'From the artist's cleaning lady', inspired by a visit to Margaret Olley Art Centre at Tweed Regional Gallery, NSW.

p. 52, 'Larkman', common in the Halifax area of Yorkshire before WW1, larks would be captured and trained to sing by enthusiasts known as larkmen. The quotation is from William Orcutt Cushing 1823-1901: 'Under his wings I am safely abiding.'

Acknowledgements

Thanks to the editors of the following venues where some of these poems first appeared:
Artemis Poetry (UK), *Best Australian Poems 2014*, *Eureka Street*, *Famous Reporter*, *Frogmore Papers* (UK), *Meniscus*, *Poetrix*, *Quadrant* and *The Canberra Times*, and in the anthologies: *Grieve 2017*, *Red Room New Shoots 2017*, *First Refuge: Poems on Social Justice*, ed. Ann Nadge (Ginnindera Press 2016), *One Last Border* (with Hazel Hall and Sandra Renew, Ginninderra Press 2015), *In Response to Triage, School of Music poets Occasional Pamphlet No 4; Stars Like Sand: Australian Speculative Poetry*, ed. Tim Jones and PS Cottier (Interactive Press 2014), *Fanfare* (Second Light Publications, UK 2015), *Australian Poetry Members Anthology 2013*, and *Fire* (Margaret River Press 2013).

'Sugihara', shortlisted, Australian Catholic University Prize 2015
'I'd drive across three moors', Highly Commended, Torriano Poetry Competition, London 2012
'Aphasia', shortlisted, Frogmore Prize, UK 2011
'At the Beaumont-Hamel Memorial, France', Winner, the Second Light Short Poem Competition, UK 2011

Owen Bullock worked with me to edit the collection and was a most attentive and close reader of my work. I thank Shane Strange from Recent Work Press for publishing this book and for his faith and confidence in me as a poet. I feel privileged to have had the opportunity to work with these generous men.

Thanks to Strathnairn Poets who've helped shape and develop some of these poems.

I thank *The Canberra Times* who published my first poem and several of the poems in this collection. And to all the editors who've published my poems and the people who've read and connected with them in some way.

I also want to pay tribute to my lovely poetry friend June Foster who passed away earlier this year. Many of the wonderful stories she told me over the years have found their way into my poems.

Thank you to Peter Bishop at Varuna who helped me to see that I am a poet. And to Maura Dooley, Stephen Knight and Bernardine Evaristo at Goldsmiths College, London.

Thanks to all the poets I've met over the past ten years or so in Canberra and other places who have inspired, affirmed, helped and given me the confidence to go on writing. It's very true what they say about Canberra. If you shake a tree, of which there many, a bunch of poets fall out. So, a big thank you to all the poets who've fallen out of the many poetry trees I've shaken ...

Finally, my thanks to Brian who's been with me and my poetry from the beginning.

Moya Pacey was born and grew up in Middlesbrough in the north of England. She came to Canberra in 1978 when it was a country town masquerading as a city and taught English until she retired in 2005. This is her second collection. Her first, *The Wardrobe* (Ginninderra Press) was runner up for the ACT Writers' Centre Poetry Award in 2010. Her poems are published widely in Australia and overseas and have appeared on buses and gallery walls, and won prizes. In 2015, she published *One Last Border: Poetry for Refugees* with Hazel Hall and Sandra Renew (Ginninderra Press). She is co-editor with Sandra Renew of the online poetry journal *Not Very Quiet*.

2016 Editions

Pulse **Prose Poetry Project**
Incantations **Subhash Jaireth**
Transit **Niloofar Fanaiyan**
Gallery of Antique Art **Paul Hetherington**
Sentences from the Archive **Jen Webb**
River's Edge **Owen Bullock**

2017 Editions

A Song, the World to Come **Miranda Lello**
Cities: Ten Poets, Ten Cities **Various**
The Bulmer Murder **Paul Munden**
Dew and Broken Glass **Penny Drysdale**
Members Only **Melinda Smith** and **Caren Florance**
the future, un-imagine **Angela Gardner** and **Caren Florance**
Proof **Maggie Shapley**
Black Tulips **Moya Pacey**
Soap **Charlotte Guest**
Isolator **Monica Carroll**
Ikaros **Paul Hetherington**
Work & Play **Owen Bullock**

all titles available from
www.recentworkpress.com

RECENT
WORK
PRESS